AI Deductions, Credits & Write-Offs

How Algorithms Find Hidden Tax Savings

By Joe Correa

Published by Live Stronger Faster

This book is for educational and informational purposes only. The author and publisher are not engaged in rendering legal, financial, tax, or other professional advice. Readers should consult a qualified professional before making any financial decisions.

First Edition

Table of Contents

Introduction

The greatest tragedy in the modern tax system is not that people pay taxes, but that they consistently pay far more than the law actually requires. Every year trillions of dollars in legally available deductions, credits, and write-offs go unclaimed simply because human beings cannot see the full financial picture clearly enough to capture them. Receipts are lost, categories are misunderstood, income streams are misclassified, and rules change faster than most taxpayers can keep up. What makes this even more painful is that the tax code itself is written to reward behavior — working, investing, raising families, owning homes, saving for retirement, starting businesses, and educating children — yet most people never fully benefit from these incentives because the system is too complex to navigate manually. Artificial intelligence changes that forever by turning every transaction, every dollar earned, and every dollar spent into an intelligent opportunity for optimization.

In the past, discovering deductions and credits was a passive, backward-looking process. A tax preparer would sit down once a year and ask a taxpayer what they spent money on, what they earned, and whether anything "special" happened. Whatever the taxpayer remembered or happened to document would be included, and everything else would simply be lost. AI replaces this flawed memory-based approach with a living, breathing financial model that continuously analyzes spending, income, and behavior in real time. Instead of guessing which deductions might apply, AI knows because it sees everything. It monitors bank accounts, credit cards, payroll deposits, investment platforms, and digital wallets and cross-references them with the entire tax code, instantly flagging any transaction that may qualify as deductible, credit-eligible, or strategically advantageous.

What makes AI so powerful in this domain is not just its ability to record data, but its ability to understand meaning. A human might see a $1,200 payment and label it simply as "software" or "equipment," but an AI system can determine whether it qualifies as a Section 179 expense, a depreciable asset, a research and development cost, a home office tool, or even a partial personal and business deduction. It understands context. It knows whether the purchase supports self-employment, rental income, investment management, education, or medical care. It knows the thresholds, limitations, phase-outs, and income-based rules that govern every deduction and credit. This transforms ordinary spending into a powerful tax-saving engine that runs continuously in the background of your life. Tax credits, in particular, are one of the most underutilized wealth tools available to individuals.

Unlike deductions, which reduce taxable income, credits reduce taxes dollar for dollar, often delivering refunds even when no tax is owed. Yet most people only claim the obvious ones, such as child tax credits or education credits, and miss dozens of others tied to energy efficiency, healthcare, caregiving, retirement contributions, dependent support, and income-based programs. AI systems are uniquely suited to capture these because they track household structure, income levels, filing status, dependents, and eligibility criteria dynamically. If your income changes, your credit eligibility changes. If a dependent ages into or out of a qualifying bracket, AI knows. If you qualify for a state-level or federal credit based on where you live or how you spend, AI detects it instantly.

Another major advantage of AI-driven deduction and credit discovery is precision. Traditional tax preparation relies on standardized forms and rough categorizations. AI uses probabilistic models and regulatory interpretation engines that continuously update as laws change. This means that when Congress introduces new credits or modifies existing ones, your AI tax engine adjusts automatically. It knows when a deduction is phased out, when a credit becomes refundable, and when new incentives are introduced for green energy, digital work, or remote employment. Instead of reading hundreds of pages of IRS publications, you have an automated compliance and optimization system working for you every day.

For self-employed individuals, gig workers, and digital entrepreneurs, the benefits multiply exponentially. Every mile driven, every phone bill, every internet charge, every piece of software, every online service, and every business-related meal becomes a potential write-off. AI tracks usage patterns, time allocation, and transaction metadata to determine what percentage of each expense qualifies for deduction. This eliminates guesswork and dramatically increases the accuracy and defensibility of your tax return. You no longer have to choose between being conservative and being optimal — AI makes it possible to be both.

AI also protects taxpayers from the most common mistake that leads to missed savings: misclassification. Many deductions and credits are lost because income is reported incorrectly or expenses are placed in the wrong category. AI understands the relationship between income sources and expenses, ensuring that deductions are matched to the correct streams. It knows how rental income interacts with depreciation, how investment expenses affect capital gains, and how business losses can offset other income. This creates a holistic tax strategy instead of a fragmented collection of forms.

As this book will show, artificial intelligence does not simply automate tax preparation — it transforms tax planning into a continuous optimization process. Every financial decision you make becomes part of a larger strategy to minimize taxes legally and maximize after-tax wealth. Whether you are a salaried employee, a freelancer, an investor, or a business owner, AI deductions and credit engines ensure that no opportunity is left on the table. In a world where every dollar matters, AI becomes the silent partner that keeps more of your hard-earned money where it belongs — in your pocket.

Chapter 1

How AI Discovers Hidden Tax Deductions and Credits

In the traditional tax world, most deductions and credits are found by accident, not design. A taxpayer remembers a receipt, a preparer asks a question, or a software program presents a checklist that happens to trigger something relevant. This random process leaves enormous amounts of money unclaimed every year. Artificial intelligence changes that by turning deduction discovery into a precision science. Instead of relying on memory or guesswork, AI builds a complete financial map of your life by continuously monitoring income, expenses, assets, and household data. Every transaction becomes a data point, and every data point is evaluated against thousands of tax rules in real time. This means that deductions are no longer something you hope to find at the end of the year — they are identified automatically as they occur.

At the heart of this system is pattern recognition. AI tax engines are trained on millions of anonymized tax returns, audit outcomes, IRS rulings, and financial records. From this training, they learn what legitimate deductions and credits look like across every income bracket, profession, and household type. When your spending or income matches a pattern that has historically produced tax savings, the system flags it. If you purchase a laptop, for example, the AI does not simply label it as an expense. It evaluates whether you are self-employed, whether you use the device for business, whether you earn income online, and whether the cost falls within depreciation or immediate write-off thresholds. The result is a far more nuanced and accurate classification than any human could produce.

One of the most powerful features of AI-driven deduction discovery is contextual awareness. Humans often struggle to separate personal and business expenses, especially in today's remote and hybrid work environments. AI, however, analyzes time, location, and usage data to determine how assets are used. If you work from home, AI can calculate the percentage of your internet, phone, utilities, and even rent or mortgage that qualifies for a home office deduction. It can see when you log into work systems, attend virtual meetings, or use productivity software, and correlate that with your spending. This creates defensible, data-backed deductions that maximize savings while minimizing audit risk.

Tax credits, which are even more valuable than deductions, benefit enormously from AI optimization. Many credits depend on income thresholds, family size, education status, energy usage, or healthcare expenses. AI continuously recalculates eligibility as your financial and personal situation changes. If your income drops or rises into a different bracket, the system updates which credits you qualify for. If a dependent turns a certain age or enters school, AI adjusts eligibility for education or child-related credits. This dynamic tracking ensures that you receive every dollar the law allows, even when your circumstances change mid-year.

Another area where AI excels is uncovering obscure or overlooked credits and deductions. The tax code contains thousands of incentives designed to encourage specific behaviors, from installing solar panels to contributing to retirement accounts, from caring for elderly relatives to working in certain industries or locations. Most people are unaware these incentives exist. AI systems, however, are built to scan the entire tax code and apply it to your data. When you make a purchase, move to a new state, change jobs, or invest in something new, the system automatically checks whether any tax benefit applies. This transforms everyday financial decisions into tax-saving opportunities.

AI also improves accuracy by eliminating human error. Manual tax preparation often leads to missed deductions because of simple mistakes — numbers are entered incorrectly, forms are overlooked, or rules are misunderstood. AI systems validate every deduction against IRS rules, historical audit data, and current regulations. If something looks inconsistent, the system flags it before filing. This reduces the risk of penalties while still allowing you to claim the maximum legally allowed savings. You get the best of both worlds: aggressive optimization and strong compliance.

As AI becomes more integrated into personal finance platforms, deduction and credit discovery will no longer be a once-a-year activity. It will happen continuously. You will be able to see, in real time, how each financial decision affects your tax outcome. Want to know how buying a new car, starting a side business, or investing in crypto will impact your taxes? AI can simulate it instantly. This predictive capability allows you to make smarter choices throughout the year, not just after it is too late.

Ultimately, AI turns the tax system from a burden into a strategic tool. Instead of dreading tax season, you gain a powerful ally that works tirelessly to reduce what you owe and increase what you keep. By discovering hidden deductions, maximizing credits, and ensuring perfect classification, AI reshapes personal taxation into a system that rewards you for every smart financial move you make.

The Algorithm That Found Emma's Missing Money

Emma had always believed she was bad with money, but in truth she was simply overwhelmed by it. Between her full-time marketing job, her freelance design clients, and her growing online shop, her finances had become a maze of bank accounts, invoices, subscriptions, and receipts scattered across apps and email folders. Every tax season she paid more than she expected, and every year her accountant would shrug and say, "You're doing fine," even though Emma felt like something was slipping through the cracks. She accepted this as normal until the day a friend introduced her to an AI-powered tax platform.

At first, Emma was skeptical. She had used tax software before, and it never felt much different from filling out forms herself. But this system was different. It connected to her bank accounts, credit cards, PayPal, Stripe, and even her freelance platforms. Within minutes, it had built a living map of her financial life. It began categorizing expenses, identifying income sources, and quietly running thousands of tax rules behind the scenes. Emma watched as numbers and categories appeared on her dashboard, revealing a financial picture she had never truly seen before.

A few weeks later, Emma received her first alert. The AI had detected that a portion of her rent qualified as a home office deduction based on her work patterns and floor space usage. Then it flagged her design software subscriptions as fully deductible business expenses. It noticed her internet and phone bills and calculated the percentage used for work. Each alert came with an explanation and a projected tax savings amount. Emma was stunned. These were expenses she had always paid, but never fully claimed.

As the year went on, the system kept working. When Emma purchased a new tablet for her design work, the AI determined whether it should be depreciated or written off immediately. When she traveled for a client meeting, it tracked mileage and meals. When she invested in an online course to improve her skills, it flagged it as an education expense. By the time tax season arrived, Emma's return was already built, optimized, and validated. The system even found credits related to her health insurance and retirement contributions that she had never known existed.

When Emma finally filed her taxes, the result felt unreal. Her refund was nearly double what it had been the previous year, even though her income had increased. There were no risky claims, no vague categories, and no guesswork — just precise, data-backed optimization. For the first time, Emma felt like the tax system was working for her instead of against her.

As she looked at the numbers on her screen, Emma realized something profound. She had not changed her spending habits or her income. The only thing that had changed was the intelligence behind how her finances were interpreted. With AI watching over every dollar, nothing was lost, nothing was forgotten, and nothing was wasted. In that moment, Emma understood that the future of taxes was not about paying less – it was about seeing more.

Chapter 2

How AI Turns Everyday Spending Into Tax-Saving Assets

Every dollar you spend tells a story, and for the tax system, that story determines whether the money is lost forever or transformed into a powerful financial advantage. In the traditional tax world, spending is treated as something that happens in the past and is loosely remembered when tax season arrives. Artificial intelligence flips this entire model by turning spending into a living, intelligent data stream that is analyzed the moment it happens. Instead of waiting for you to categorize expenses months later, AI evaluates transactions in real time, identifying which purchases qualify as business expenses, investment costs, medical deductions, education write-offs, or household credits. This real-time intelligence ensures that nothing falls through the cracks and that every eligible dollar is captured with precision.

One of the greatest strengths of AI is its ability to interpret context. When you buy a computer, for example, AI does not simply record a purchase — it examines how you use that device. It looks at login activity, software usage, work schedules, and income sources to determine whether the device supports business operations, creative work, investment management, or personal entertainment. That context allows the system to assign the correct tax treatment automatically. A purchase that might have been partially deductible or completely ignored in the past is now properly classified and optimized, often generating significant savings that a human would never detect.

AI also excels at handling blended personal and professional expenses, which are increasingly common in modern life. Home internet, mobile phones, vehicles, and even living space are often used for both work and personal activities. Instead of forcing you to guess or rely on rough percentages, AI uses behavioral data to calculate precise usage ratios. It can see how often your phone is used for business calls, how many hours your internet supports work activity, or how frequently your vehicle is driven for professional purposes. These insights create defensible, highly accurate deductions that maximize tax savings while reducing audit risk.

Another powerful advantage of AI-driven expense analysis is its ability to connect spending to income generation. The tax code rewards investments that produce income, and AI understands these relationships in extraordinary detail. If you pay for marketing, software, training, or equipment that increases your earning potential, the system recognizes this and applies the appropriate tax treatment. It knows how expenses relate to freelance income, rental income, investment gains, and even digital product sales. This holistic understanding turns your entire financial life into a coordinated tax strategy rather than a collection of disconnected transactions.

AI also continuously adapts to changes in tax law. When new deductions, credits, or depreciation rules are introduced, the system updates automatically. This means that spending which might not have qualified for a benefit last year could qualify this year without you having to learn anything new. The AI simply applies the new rules to your data and captures the benefit. This eliminates the lag between law changes and taxpayer awareness that has historically caused people to miss out on valuable incentives.

Perhaps most importantly, AI removes fear from the deduction process. Many people avoid claiming legitimate expenses because they are afraid of being audited or making a mistake. AI solves this by validating every deduction against IRS rules, historical audit data, and documentation. It keeps digital records, receipts, and usage data to support every claim. This gives taxpayers the confidence to claim everything they are entitled to without crossing any legal lines.

As AI becomes embedded in financial platforms, spending itself becomes a strategic activity. You will be able to see how purchases affect your tax outcome before you even make them. Want to know whether buying new equipment, upgrading your home office, or investing in a course will reduce your taxes? AI can tell you instantly. This transforms financial decisions from guesswork into informed, optimized actions.

In this new world, money is never just spent — it is deployed. Every transaction becomes a potential asset, every purchase a possible deduction, and every investment a step toward greater after-tax wealth. AI does not just record what you do; it turns what you do into something that works for you, silently and relentlessly improving your financial future.

The Receipt That Changed Carlos's Life

Carlos had always run his small landscaping business with pride, but not with much financial clarity. He worked long days, paid his workers, bought equipment, and covered fuel, but when tax season came, his profits seemed to vanish. His accountant would tell him he owed thousands, and Carlos never quite understood why. He knew he spent a lot to keep the business running, yet it felt like none of it mattered when the IRS came calling.

Everything changed when Carlos started using an AI-powered tax system recommended by a fellow business owner. The system connected to his bank account and credit card and immediately began categorizing every transaction. Fuel purchases were tagged to his trucks, equipment was logged as depreciable assets, and even his work boots and safety gear were classified as deductible. The AI even tracked mileage through his phone and compared it to his job locations.

One day, Carlos received an alert that stunned him. The AI had discovered that a portion of his home qualified as a business storage and office space, making part of his rent and utilities deductible. He had never even considered that before. Then it found that many of his tool purchases could be written off faster under updated depreciation rules. Each discovery came with documentation and explanations that made everything clear and safe.

By the time tax season arrived, Carlos's financial picture had completely changed. His taxable income was far lower, not because he earned less, but because the AI had finally captured what he had always been spending. His tax bill dropped dramatically, freeing up money he could use to expand his business. For the first time, Carlos felt in control.

As he looked at his optimized return, Carlos realized that the problem had never been his business — it had been the way his spending was being understood. With AI watching every dollar, nothing was invisible anymore. What once felt like money lost had become money working for him, and that made all the difference.

Chapter 3

How AI Prevents Overpayment and Maximizes Legal Tax Savings

One of the most expensive mistakes taxpayers make is not filing incorrectly, but filing incompletely. Overpayment is far more common than underpayment, yet it is rarely discussed because the IRS does not warn you when you give them too much. In fact, the system quietly benefits from every missed deduction, overlooked credit, and misclassified expense. Artificial intelligence changes this imbalance by treating tax optimization as a continuous financial audit of your own money. Instead of waiting until filing season to discover what was lost, AI tracks your financial activity throughout the year, measuring what you should owe versus what you are likely to owe based on current behavior. This creates an early warning system for overpayment, allowing adjustments long before it is too late.

At the core of this system is predictive modeling. AI does not merely record what has happened; it forecasts what will happen if nothing changes. By analyzing income trends, spending patterns, and withholding rates, the system can estimate your year-end tax liability months in advance. If the model predicts that you will overpay, AI recommends actions to rebalance your finances. This might include adjusting withholding, increasing retirement contributions, accelerating deductible purchases, or restructuring income timing. Instead of discovering a refund after filing, you get the money in your pocket throughout the year when it matters most.

AI also prevents overpayment by eliminating the hidden inefficiencies that plague traditional tax preparation. Many taxpayers are placed in default withholding categories that do not match their real financial situation. Bonuses, side income, investment gains, and freelance work can all distort withholding, causing far more tax to be taken out than necessary. AI monitors all income sources in real time and compares them against your total tax profile. When it sees a mismatch, it alerts you and provides precise recommendations for correction, ensuring that your money is not unnecessarily tied up with the government.

Another major source of overpayment comes from fear. Many people deliberately under-claim deductions because they are worried about audits, penalties, or making mistakes. AI eliminates this fear by validating every optimization against IRS rules, historical audit data, and legal precedents. It knows which deductions are commonly audited, which are safe, and how to document everything properly. This allows you to claim the full amount you are entitled to without risking compliance issues. You are no longer guessing where the line is — AI shows you exactly where it lies.

AI also understands the complex interactions between different parts of the tax code. Many deductions and credits are reduced or eliminated when income crosses certain thresholds. Humans often miss these phase-outs or apply them incorrectly. AI models these interactions continuously, ensuring that your financial decisions do not accidentally push you into a less favorable tax position. It can even simulate alternative scenarios, showing you how shifting income, expenses, or investments could reduce your total tax burden.

Perhaps most importantly, AI ensures that optimization happens at the right time. Timing is everything in taxation. Whether income is earned in December or January, whether an expense is paid before or after year-end, and whether an asset is sold this year or next can have enormous tax consequences. AI tracks these timing opportunities and alerts you when strategic moves could save you money. This turns tax planning into a proactive, year-round activity instead of a reactive scramble.

In a world powered by artificial intelligence, paying too much tax becomes a choice rather than a mistake. With continuous monitoring, predictive modeling, and rule-based optimization,

AI ensures that every dollar you earn is taxed only as much as the law requires — and not a penny more. This is the true promise of AI-powered tax optimization: not just compliance, but financial control.

The Refund Daniel Never Had to Wait For

Daniel had always looked forward to his tax refund, but he never understood why he had to wait so long to get it. Every year, thousands of dollars were withheld from his paychecks, only to be returned months later after he filed. It felt like he was giving the government an interest-free loan, but he did not know how to change it. When his company introduced an AI-powered financial platform as part of their benefits package, Daniel decided to try it.

The system quickly analyzed his salary, bonuses, investment income, and side consulting work. Within days, it told him something surprising: he was on track to overpay his taxes by nearly eight thousand dollars that year. The AI showed him exactly why — his withholding was based only on his salary, not his total financial picture. It then calculated the optimal withholding amount and guided him through adjusting his payroll settings.

As the months passed, Daniel noticed his paychecks growing slightly larger. The extra money allowed him to pay down debt and start saving more aggressively. Meanwhile, the AI kept monitoring his income and spending, making small adjustments whenever something changed. When he received a bonus, it recalculated his tax position. When he made a big purchase, it checked for deductions. Nothing was left to chance.

When tax season finally arrived, Daniel was shocked to see that he owed almost nothing and received only a tiny refund. But instead of feeling disappointed, he felt empowered. He realized that he had already received his money throughout the year, exactly when he needed it. The AI had turned his finances into a perfectly balanced system.

Looking back, Daniel saw how different his life had become simply by understanding his taxes in real time. He was no longer waiting for a refund to rescue him. With AI guiding every decision, his money was finally working for him instead of sitting idle in someone else's account.

Chapter 4

How AI Eliminates Guesswork and Creates Bulletproof Tax Accuracy

Accuracy has always been the silent dividing line between tax confidence and tax anxiety. Most taxpayers are not intentionally careless; they are simply forced to make decisions with incomplete information. They guess how much of an expense is deductible, estimate percentages, round numbers, and hope the software or preparer catches mistakes. Artificial intelligence eliminates this uncertainty by replacing assumptions with evidence. Every calculation, classification, and deduction is supported by data, behavioral patterns, and continuously updated tax logic. Accuracy is no longer a matter of trust or intuition — it is engineered into the system itself.

At the foundation of AI-driven tax accuracy is data integration. Traditional tax preparation relies on fragmented inputs: a few bank statements, a stack of receipts, and whatever information the taxpayer remembers to share. AI systems, by contrast, connect directly to financial institutions, payment processors, payroll platforms, investment accounts, and digital wallets. This creates a unified financial timeline where every dollar earned and spent is accounted for. Missing information becomes immediately visible, and inconsistencies are flagged automatically. Instead of discovering errors months later through IRS notices, issues are resolved in real time.

AI also excels at classification accuracy, which is one of the most common failure points in manual tax preparation. Misclassified income or expenses can quietly distort an entire tax return. AI uses layered classification models that analyze transaction descriptions, vendor data, usage patterns, timing, and historical behavior. A single expense is not categorized once — it is evaluated multiple times across different rule sets to ensure it is placed in the most accurate and beneficial category allowed by law. This multi-pass verification dramatically reduces errors while maximizing legitimate tax benefits.

Another critical advantage of AI accuracy is rule consistency. Human preparers interpret rules differently, and even software-driven systems often rely on static decision trees. AI systems operate using adaptive rule engines that update continuously as regulations change. When the IRS issues new guidance, court rulings clarify interpretations, or thresholds are adjusted, AI models incorporate these changes automatically. This ensures that every calculation reflects the most current legal framework, not last year's assumptions or outdated templates. Documentation is another area where AI transforms accuracy into protection. Every deduction, credit, and adjustment is supported by digital records that are automatically stored and linked. Receipts are captured, categorized, and associated with the correct tax treatment. Usage data supports percentage-based deductions. Income sources are reconciled across platforms to ensure consistency. If questions arise, the documentation already exists. This removes the panic of scrambling for proof and replaces it with calm, organized readiness.

AI also detects errors that humans often miss because they exist across multiple parts of a return. For example, an income adjustment might reduce eligibility for a credit, or a deduction in one category might affect limitations elsewhere. AI models these interactions continuously, ensuring that optimizing one area does not accidentally create problems in another. This holistic validation is nearly impossible to replicate manually, especially for taxpayers with complex financial lives.

Perhaps most importantly, AI eliminates emotional bias from tax decisions. Fear, uncertainty, and misunderstanding often lead people to under-claim or misreport. AI has no fear. It applies rules exactly as written and supported by data. This creates returns that are both maximally optimized and defensible. Accuracy becomes not just about avoiding mistakes, but about confidently claiming what you are entitled to. As tax systems grow more complex and financial lives more digital, accuracy becomes a competitive advantage. AI delivers that advantage by transforming tax preparation from a stressful annual event into a precise, continuously verified financial process. When accuracy is automated, confidence follows — and confidence is the foundation of long-term financial control.

The Seven-Year Silence That Finally Broke

For seven years, Nina lived with a quiet, persistent fear that followed her every tax season. She never talked about it, never admitted it out loud, but it was always there — the fear that she had done something wrong. Nina worked as a remote project manager, earned income from multiple clients, invested modestly, and shared expenses with her partner. Every year, she filed her taxes carefully, double-checking numbers, saving receipts, and hoping she had not missed something important. The silence from the IRS felt less like reassurance and more like a ticking clock.

What Nina did not realize was that her anxiety came from uncertainty, not risk. She did not know whether her deductions were accurate, whether her income was classified correctly, or whether her percentages made sense. She had guessed her way through too many decisions because no one had ever shown her a better way. When a colleague recommended an AI-powered tax platform, Nina hesitated.

She worried that connecting everything would expose mistakes she had unknowingly made. Eventually, curiosity outweighed fear, and she signed up.

The first thing the system did was build a complete financial map of her life. It connected to her bank accounts, payroll deposits, freelance invoices, investment platforms, and expense cards. Within minutes, it showed her a timeline of every dollar moving in and out of her world. Nina stared at the screen in disbelief. For the first time, her finances were not scattered — they were unified. The system immediately flagged inconsistencies she had never noticed: duplicated income entries, expenses categorized differently across years, and percentages that did not align with actual usage patterns.

Instead of panicking, Nina watched as the AI explained each issue calmly. It recalculated her home office usage based on work hours, device activity, and internet usage. It reclassified several expenses she had under-claimed out of caution. It reconciled her investment income with brokerage reports and adjusted carryovers she had misunderstood for years. Nothing was dramatic or accusatory. It was methodical, precise, and unemotional.

As weeks passed, Nina began to feel something unfamiliar — relief. Every transaction now had a place. Every deduction had support. Every number had a reason. The system stored receipts automatically, linked them to categories, and documented usage patterns. Nina no longer worried about whether she could explain her return. She could, down to the smallest detail, because the explanation already existed.

Then came the moment she had secretly feared for years: an IRS notice arrived in the mail. Her hands shook as she opened it. But instead of panic, she logged into the AI platform. The notice referenced a discrepancy in reported income from several years earlier. Within seconds, the system pulled up the exact transactions, the reconciliation logic, and the documentation. It generated a clear response explaining the issue, supported by records Nina did not even know she had. She mailed the response with confidence.

Weeks later, another letter arrived. The issue was resolved. No penalties. No changes. No further action required. Nina sat quietly at her kitchen table, holding the paper, and felt a weight lift that she had carried for nearly a decade. The fear had never been about the IRS — it had been about not knowing. AI had given her something far more valuable than savings or refunds. It had given her certainty.

From that day on, tax season no longer arrived with dread. It arrived like a routine check-in, calm and predictable. Nina understood then that accuracy was not about being perfect. It was about being supported. With AI watching every detail, the silence was no longer threatening — it was peaceful.

Chapter 5

How AI Coordinates Deductions Across Your Entire Financial Life

The final and most powerful advantage of artificial intelligence in tax optimization is not found in any single deduction or credit, but in coordination. Most taxpayers unknowingly treat their finances as separate silos: income here, expenses there, investments somewhere else, and household decisions in an entirely different mental category. The tax code, however, does not operate in silos. Every dollar interacts with every other dollar through thresholds, phaseouts, limitations, carryforwards, and timing rules. Artificial intelligence is uniquely capable of understanding these interactions simultaneously, transforming isolated deductions into a unified, optimized tax strategy.

In a traditional tax setup, deductions are often claimed independently without regard for their combined effect. A taxpayer may take a retirement deduction without realizing it pushes them below a credit threshold, or claim an expense that reduces eligibility for another benefit. Humans struggle with these cascading effects because they require tracking dozens of variables at once. AI thrives in this environment. It models the entire tax system as a dynamic network, recalculating outcomes every time a variable changes. This means your deductions are no longer optimized individually — they are optimized collectively.

One of the most important coordination challenges involves income timing and expense timing. Whether income is recognized this year or next, whether expenses are paid in December or January, and whether assets are depreciated quickly or slowly can dramatically alter tax outcomes. AI continuously evaluates these timing decisions in real time. If accelerating an expense improves your overall position without harming future benefits, the system flags it. If delaying income preserves eligibility for a valuable credit, AI identifies that window. This level of coordination turns tax planning into a strategic calendar rather than a once-a-year calculation.

Household coordination is another area where AI delivers massive value. Many deductions and credits depend on filing status, dependent status, shared expenses, and combined income. AI models households as financial ecosystems rather than individual filers. It understands how expenses should be allocated between spouses, how dependents affect multiple credits simultaneously, and how shared assets impact deductions. This eliminates guesswork and prevents costly misallocations that reduce total household benefits. AI also coordinates deductions across multiple income streams. In today's economy, it is common for one person to earn W-2 income, 1099 income, investment income, and passive income simultaneously. Each category has its own rules, limitations, and opportunities. AI understands how expenses attach to specific income sources and how losses in one area can offset gains in another. It ensures that deductions are applied where they produce the greatest benefit while remaining compliant. This holistic approach often unlocks savings that are completely invisible when income streams are treated separately.

Another critical coordination function involves carryforwards and long-term planning. Many deductions and credits cannot be fully used in a single year. Losses, depreciation, education credits, and investment-related benefits often carry forward into future years. AI tracks these continuously, ensuring they are not forgotten or misapplied. More importantly, it integrates them into future projections, allowing you to make decisions today that optimize not just this year's taxes, but the next five, ten, or even twenty years.

AI also coordinates state and federal tax strategies. Tax rules vary dramatically by location, and actions that reduce federal tax may increase state tax, or vice versa. AI models both systems simultaneously, ensuring that optimization is balanced rather than one-sided. This is especially valuable for taxpayers who move, work remotely, or earn income across multiple jurisdictions. The result is a strategy that maximizes total after-tax income, not just one piece of the puzzle.

Ultimately, AI coordination transforms deductions from a reactive checklist into a proactive financial strategy. Your taxes are no longer something that happens to you — they are something that is continuously managed on your behalf. By synchronizing income, expenses, assets, household structure, and timing, AI creates a level of optimization that no human, no matter how skilled, could replicate consistently. This is the future of personal taxation: not isolated savings, but total financial alignment.

The Year Everything Finally Made Sense

For most of her adult life, Lauren felt like she was running a financial relay race where no one ever handed her the baton. She earned a solid salary as a healthcare administrator, ran a small online coaching business on the side, owned a rental condo with her brother, and was raising two children with her spouse. On paper, she was successful. In reality, her finances felt fragmented and confusing. Every year, tax season left her with the same question: *How can I be doing everything right and still feel like I'm losing money?*

Lauren had a tax preparer she trusted, but even he admitted that her situation was "complex." Forms multiplied every year. One decision seemed to cancel out another. A credit she expected would disappear because her income was slightly too high. A deduction would help on one side but hurt on another. It felt like a game with invisible rules that changed just as she thought she understood them.

The turning point came when Lauren decided to try an AI-powered tax system after a particularly frustrating filing season. She didn't expect miracles. She just wanted clarity. When she connected her accounts, the system began doing something no one had ever done for her before — it showed her how everything was connected. Not just income and expenses, but timing, household decisions, investments, and future consequences.

The AI showed her that claiming a particular deduction aggressively in one area was quietly reducing her eligibility for a valuable child-related credit. It demonstrated how shifting income from her side business by just a few weeks could preserve that credit without changing her total earnings. It revealed that depreciation on the rental condo was being used inefficiently and could be restructured to benefit both her and her brother more evenly. For the first time, Lauren wasn't just seeing numbers — she was seeing relationships. As the year progressed, the system guided her decisions gently but consistently. When she considered buying new equipment for her coaching business, it showed how the timing would affect both federal and state taxes. When she adjusted her retirement contributions, it recalculated how that change interacted with multiple credits and deductions simultaneously. When her spouse received a bonus, the AI updated projections instantly, showing how to rebalance withholding and expenses to stay optimized.

What struck Lauren most was how calm everything felt. There were no surprises, no last-minute scrambling, no "we'll see what happens at tax time." She could open her dashboard at any moment and see exactly where she stood — not just for this year, but for years ahead. Carryforwards were tracked. Phaseouts were anticipated. Nothing was accidental anymore.

At the end of the year, Lauren sat down to review her return before filing. It was the cleanest, most logical tax picture she had ever seen. Every deduction made sense in context. Every credit fit into a larger strategy. The outcome wasn't just a lower tax bill — it was confidence. She finally understood why each decision mattered and how it fit into the whole.

That night, after the kids were asleep, Lauren closed her laptop and smiled. For the first time in years, her finances felt aligned. Not perfect, not static, but coherent. AI hadn't just saved her money. It had given her something far more valuable — a sense that the system finally made sense, and that she was no longer navigating it alone.

Chapter 6

How AI Handles Complex Assets, Investments, and Multi-Layered Tax Scenarios

As personal finances evolve beyond simple wages and savings accounts, taxes stop being linear and start becoming multidimensional. Assets such as real estate, cryptocurrency, stocks, retirement accounts, equity compensation, and digital income streams each follow their own tax logic, timelines, and reporting requirements. When these assets interact, complexity compounds rapidly. Human-based tax preparation struggles here not because of incompetence, but because the cognitive load is overwhelming. Artificial intelligence was built for exactly this kind of environment. It thrives where multiple systems intersect, rules overlap, and outcomes depend on timing, classification, and long-term planning rather than single-year snapshots.

AI approaches complex assets by modeling them as living financial entities rather than static line items. A rental property, for example, is not just income and expenses. It includes depreciation schedules, capital improvements, passive activity rules, loss limitations, carryforwards, local tax rules, and eventual exit strategies. AI tracks all of these dimensions simultaneously. It knows when depreciation should be accelerated or slowed, how rental losses interact with other income, and how improvements affect future capital gains. When you refinance, sell, or exchange a property, the AI recalculates the entire historical chain instantly, ensuring that nothing is missed and nothing is misapplied.

Cryptocurrency introduces an even higher level of complexity due to its transactional nature. Every trade, swap, transfer, reward, and staking event can trigger tax consequences. Manual tracking is nearly impossible at scale. AI systems ingest transaction histories from wallets, exchanges, and blockchains directly, reconstructing cost basis, holding periods, and gains with forensic precision. They understand the difference between taxable events and non-taxable transfers, between short-term and long-term gains, and between income and appreciation. As regulations evolve, AI updates classification logic automatically, ensuring compliance without sacrificing optimization.

Investment portfolios also benefit enormously from AI coordination. Capital gains, dividends, interest income, and losses all interact with tax brackets, credits, and deductions. AI continuously monitors portfolios and models tax-efficient strategies such as loss harvesting, gain timing, and asset location. It knows when selling an asset will push income into a higher bracket or phase out a credit, and when waiting could preserve long-term gains treatment. Instead of reacting after trades are made, AI informs decisions before they happen.

Equity compensation adds another layer of difficulty. Stock options, restricted stock units, employee stock purchase plans, and performance shares all follow unique tax rules that depend on vesting schedules, exercise timing, and market value. AI models these variables dynamically. It can show the tax impact of exercising now versus later, holding versus selling, and how equity income interacts with overall tax exposure. This allows individuals to align career decisions with tax strategy rather than being blindsided by unexpected liabilities.

Retirement accounts further complicate matters with contribution limits, deduction eligibility, distribution rules, and penalties. AI tracks contributions across accounts, monitors eligibility based on income, and models future required minimum distributions. It understands how retirement planning intersects with current tax optimization, ensuring that short-term savings do not create long-term tax traps.

What makes AI indispensable in complex scenarios is not just its ability to calculate, but its ability to coordinate across time. Many asset-related tax decisions have consequences that unfold over decades. AI builds multi-year projections that account for growth, rule changes, and life events. This transforms tax planning from a backward-looking compliance task into a forward-looking wealth strategy.

In a financial world filled with complexity, AI does not simplify by ignoring details — it simplifies by mastering them. It brings order to chaos, clarity to confusion, and strategy to situations that once felt unmanageable. For anyone with assets beyond a paycheck, AI is no longer optional. It is the only tool capable of seeing the full picture.

The Map Beneath the Numbers

Ethan always thought he was financially savvy. He invested early, diversified his portfolio, bought a rental property in his thirties, and dabbled in crypto long before most people knew what a blockchain was. On the surface, his finances looked impressive. Beneath the surface, they were tangled. Every year, tax season arrived like a storm he prepared for but never fully understood. He paid what he was told, filed what was required, and assumed the rest was just the price of complexity.

The problem wasn't that Ethan lacked discipline. It was that no one — not his accountant, not his software, not even Ethan himself — could see how everything interacted. His rental losses didn't seem to help his taxes as much as he expected. His crypto gains created unexpected liabilities. His stock sales sometimes resulted in surprisingly high bills, even in years when his income hadn't changed much. It felt arbitrary, as if the rules were shifting without warning.

When a friend suggested an AI-powered tax platform designed for complex assets, Ethan hesitated. He had tried advanced tools before, and they always promised clarity but delivered more forms. Still, curiosity won. He connected his brokerage accounts, rental property records, crypto wallets, and retirement accounts. Then he waited.

What appeared on his screen was not a report, but a map.

The AI visualized his entire financial life across time. It showed how depreciation from his rental property flowed forward year after year, how unused losses stacked quietly in the background, and how certain investment gains were pushing him just over critical income thresholds. It revealed that some of his crypto trades had been taxed as ordinary income when they could have been treated differently if timed more carefully. It showed how equity compensation from his employer had quietly inflated his tax bracket without him realizing it.

For the first time, Ethan could see cause and effect.

The system didn't scold him. It didn't overwhelm him. It explained. It showed alternative timelines — what would have happened if he had delayed a sale, exercised an option later, or structured improvements on his rental differently. The numbers changed in front of him, not as abstractions, but as outcomes tied to decisions.

As the year progressed, Ethan began using the AI as a guide rather than a calculator. Before making a trade, he checked the projected impact. Before investing in another property, he explored different ownership and depreciation scenarios. When crypto regulations shifted, the system adapted instantly, reclassifying past transactions without panic or guesswork.

The real transformation came during tax season. Instead of anxiety, Ethan felt calm. The return wasn't just accurate — it was logical. Every number told a story he understood. Every outcome matched a decision he remembered making intentionally.

One evening, Ethan sat at his desk, scrolling through the multi-year projection the AI had built for him. It wasn't just about taxes anymore. It was about direction. For years, he had been moving forward without a map, trusting instinct and hoping the system would catch up. Now, the map was clear, detailed, and alive. He realized then that complexity had never been the enemy. Blindness had. With AI illuminating the path beneath the numbers, Ethan finally felt like he was steering his financial future — not just surviving it.

Chapter 7

How AI Forecasts Taxes, Optimizes Withholding, and Eliminates Year-End Surprises

For most people, tax season feels like judgment day. No matter how organized they are, the final outcome often comes as a surprise — owing far more than expected or receiving a refund that feels random and poorly timed. This uncertainty is not a personal failure; it is a structural flaw in how taxes have traditionally been managed. Taxes are dynamic, yet most systems treat them as static. Artificial intelligence corrects this mismatch by transforming taxes from a backward-looking calculation into a forward-looking forecast that evolves in real time alongside your financial life.

At the core of AI-powered tax forecasting is continuous visibility. Instead of waiting until the end of the year to total income and expenses, AI tracks them as they happen. Every paycheck, bonus, side-income deposit, investment gain, and deductible expense updates your projected tax liability instantly. The system maintains a rolling estimate of what you will owe — not just today, but at year-end if nothing changes. This living forecast becomes the foundation for proactive decision-making rather than reactive damage control.

Withholding optimization is one of the most immediate benefits of this forecasting capability. Many taxpayers unknowingly over-withhold, effectively lending money to the government interest-free, while others under-withhold and face penalties or stressful payment plans. AI analyzes your complete income picture, not just your primary job, and compares it against your current withholding setup. When discrepancies appear, the system calculates precise adjustments to bring withholding into balance. The goal is not a large refund or a painful bill, but near-perfect alignment – keeping your money in your hands throughout the year without risking underpayment.

AI forecasting also adapts instantly to life changes. A raise, job change, new side business, investment sale, or major expense can dramatically alter tax outcomes. Traditional systems catch these changes too late. AI catches them immediately. When income spikes, the system recalculates projected liability and suggests adjustments. When deductions increase, it recalibrates withholding downward. This responsiveness ensures that no single event derails your entire tax plan.

Another critical advantage of AI forecasting is its ability to model scenarios. Instead of guessing how a decision might affect your taxes, you can see the outcome before you act. Want to know whether contributing more to retirement will reduce your tax bill enough to matter? AI shows you. Considering selling an asset? The system compares selling now versus later, factoring in brackets, credits, and long-term impacts. This predictive insight turns tax planning into a strategic exercise rather than a leap of faith.

AI also accounts for psychological and cash-flow realities. While minimizing taxes is important, liquidity matters too. AI balances tax efficiency with monthly cash needs, ensuring that withholding adjustments do not create financial strain. It understands that taxes exist within the broader context of life — bills, savings goals, investments, and emergencies. This holistic awareness allows it to recommend strategies that are not just mathematically optimal, but practically sustainable.

Perhaps most importantly, AI forecasting eliminates fear. Fear of owing, fear of penalties, fear of being unprepared. When you can see your tax position clearly at all times, there is no mystery. Adjustments become routine, not urgent. Decisions become informed, not anxious. Tax season loses its emotional charge and becomes a simple checkpoint rather than a reckoning.

In an AI-powered system, surprises disappear because uncertainty disappears. Taxes stop being something that happens *to* you and become something that is managed *with* you, quietly and continuously. Forecasting is the bridge between compliance and control, and AI is the only tool capable of maintaining that bridge in real time.

December Without Fear

For as long as she could remember, December had been Sofia's most stressful month — and not because of holidays. Every year, as the calendar crept toward year-end, a familiar knot formed in her stomach. She earned good money as a product manager, supplemented her income with consulting work, and invested steadily. Yet taxes always felt unpredictable. Some years she owed thousands. Other years she received refunds she didn't understand. No matter the outcome, the waiting and uncertainty drained her.

Sofia was responsible in every other area of her life. She budgeted carefully, saved consistently, and planned ahead. Taxes were the one area that refused to cooperate with her sense of order. Her accountant told her, "We'll know when we know," and that answer never sat right with her. She wanted clarity *before* the bill arrived, not after.

Everything changed the year Sofia adopted an AI-powered tax forecasting system. At first, it felt almost too simple. She connected her payroll, consulting income, investment accounts, and expenses. The system processed silently for a moment, then displayed a single number: her projected year-end tax liability if nothing changed. It wasn't alarming — but it wasn't comfortable either. What startled her most was not the number, but the confidence behind it. The system showed her exactly how it arrived there, tracing income streams, deductions, and thresholds with calm precision.

As the weeks passed, Sofia began checking her dashboard the way she once checked the weather. Not obsessively — just enough to stay oriented. When she received a consulting payment larger than expected, the projection adjusted instantly. The AI notified her that if she did nothing, she would under-withhold slightly by year-end. It offered three options: adjust payroll withholding, set aside estimated payments, or increase a retirement contribution. Each option showed its effect on both her taxes and her monthly cash flow.

For the first time, Sofia felt like she was choosing rather than reacting.

In late summer, her company announced bonuses would be paid earlier than usual. The AI recalculated her projections within minutes and alerted her that this timing would push more income into the current year than expected. It suggested small withholding changes spread over several months to absorb the impact smoothly. Sofia followed the guidance, barely noticing the difference in her paycheck – but watching her projected tax balance stabilize felt like magic.

Then December arrived.

In previous years, December meant dread. This year, it meant clarity. Sofia already knew, within a narrow range, exactly what her tax outcome would be. There were no frantic last-minute deductions, no desperate questions, no sleepless nights wondering what surprise awaited her in April. When she reviewed her dashboard, the numbers were steady, familiar, and unsurprising.

On a quiet evening just before the holidays, Sofia sat with a cup of tea and reflected on how different the season felt. The stress she had normalized for years was gone. Not reduced – gone. She hadn't earned less. She hadn't worked harder. She hadn't become a tax expert. She had simply been given visibility.

When tax season eventually arrived, the return matched the forecast almost perfectly. There was no shock, no disappointment, no relief – just confirmation. Sofia smiled as she submitted the filing, not because she was done, but because she had never felt *done* all year. She had felt prepared.

That December, Sofia realized something quietly profound: peace doesn't come from avoiding problems. It comes from seeing them clearly long before they arrive. With AI forecasting her taxes in real time, fear had lost its power — and December had finally become just another month.

Chapter 8

How AI Stays Compliant, Adapts to Tax Law Changes, and Keeps You Protected

Tax law is not static. It evolves constantly, shaped by legislation, regulatory guidance, court rulings, administrative updates, and economic policy shifts. For the average taxpayer, this constant motion creates an impossible challenge. Rules change faster than people can learn them, and by the time new information becomes widely understood, it is often already outdated. This is one of the greatest structural weaknesses of traditional tax preparation: it assumes that humans can keep pace with a system designed to change continuously. Artificial intelligence resolves this imbalance by making adaptability the core feature of compliance rather than an afterthought.

At the foundation of AI-driven compliance is real-time rule ingestion. Modern AI tax systems are connected to legislative updates, IRS publications, Treasury guidance, and judicial interpretations as they are released. Instead of waiting for annual software updates or relying on preparers to interpret changes manually, AI integrates new rules into its decision logic immediately. This means that when a deduction threshold changes, a credit is expanded or restricted, or a reporting requirement is modified, your tax strategy adjusts automatically. Compliance is no longer reactive; it is always current.

AI also understands that tax law is not just a list of rules, but a system of interpretation. Many provisions contain gray areas where intent, usage, and documentation matter. AI models are trained on historical enforcement data, audit outcomes, and court decisions, allowing them to distinguish between aggressive but defensible positions and risky interpretations likely to trigger scrutiny. This contextual awareness allows AI to optimize within the law while avoiding unnecessary exposure. You are not just compliant on paper — you are compliant in practice.

Another critical advantage of AI compliance is consistency. Human error often arises from inconsistency: a deduction claimed one year but not another, income categorized differently across periods, or documentation handled unevenly. These inconsistencies can raise red flags even when individual items are legitimate. AI eliminates this problem by maintaining continuity across years. It tracks historical filings, compares them to current data, and ensures that changes are logical, documented, and aligned with known life events. This continuity reduces audit risk while strengthening long-term accuracy. Documentation management is another area where AI excels. Compliance is not just about doing the right thing —

it is about proving it. AI automatically collects, stores, and links documentation to every deduction, credit, and adjustment. Receipts are captured digitally, usage data is logged, and explanatory notes are generated automatically. If rules require substantiation, the substantiation already exists. This turns compliance from a stressful burden into a passive byproduct of normal financial activity.

AI also adapts to jurisdictional complexity. Federal rules interact with state and local tax laws in ways that are difficult to manage manually. AI systems model these layers simultaneously, ensuring that compliance is maintained across all relevant jurisdictions. When state rules diverge from federal treatment, AI accounts for those differences automatically. This is especially valuable for remote workers, investors, and individuals with multi-state exposure, where compliance errors are both common and costly.

Perhaps most importantly, AI reframes compliance as protection rather than restriction. Traditional tax advice often emphasizes what *not* to do out of fear of penalties. AI focuses on what *can* be done safely within the rules. By understanding enforcement patterns and regulatory intent, AI enables confident optimization without crossing legal boundaries. Compliance becomes a shield that enables opportunity rather than a barrier that limits it.

In an increasingly complex tax environment, compliance is no longer about memorizing rules. It is about having a system that evolves as fast as the law itself. AI provides that system. It watches, learns, adapts, and protects – silently ensuring that your financial life remains aligned with the rules, no matter how often they change.

The Letter That Never Came

Marcus had built his life on responsibility. He followed the rules, paid his bills on time, and avoided unnecessary risks. Yet when it came to taxes, a quiet anxiety lingered beneath his calm exterior. He worked as a remote engineer, invested in index funds, occasionally traded stocks, and had recently started renting out a room in his home. None of it felt reckless, but it all felt *exposed.* Every article he read about audits and penalties reinforced the idea that one missed rule could undo years of careful planning.

Marcus's fear wasn't dramatic. It was subtle and persistent. Each year after filing, he would wait. Weeks would pass, then months. No news should have meant good news, but silence felt ominous. He half-expected a letter to arrive at any time, informing him that something had been misunderstood, misapplied, or misreported. When a colleague mentioned an AI-powered tax system designed to track rule changes automatically, Marcus listened more closely than he wanted to admit.

He started using the system cautiously, connecting only a few accounts at first. What surprised him was how little it asked of him. The AI didn't bombard him with questions or warnings. It simply observed. It pulled in income, expenses, investment activity, and rental records, then quietly compared everything against current tax law. When it finished its initial analysis, it didn't say he was wrong. It said he was *inconsistent*.

The system showed Marcus that a rental-related expense had been treated differently across two years, not because the rules changed, but because his previous software had categorized it differently. It flagged a reporting threshold that had quietly shifted the previous year, altering how certain investment income should be disclosed. It explained, calmly and clearly, what had changed in the law and why his situation now required a slightly different approach.

Marcus felt a strange mix of discomfort and relief. Discomfort because he realized how easily these changes could have gone unnoticed. Relief because they hadn't.

As months passed, Marcus began to trust the system. When new tax guidance was released related to remote work deductions, the AI adjusted his classifications automatically. When state rules changed around rental income reporting, the system recalculated his exposure without him lifting a finger. Each adjustment came with an explanation, not a warning. It felt less like being corrected and more like being guided.

Then one spring afternoon, Marcus received a notification – not from the IRS, but from the AI. It informed him that a commonly misunderstood deduction had been clarified by recent court rulings and that his prior treatment was now even more defensible. The system updated its documentation automatically, strengthening his compliance profile retroactively. Marcus leaned back in his chair, realizing something important: compliance wasn't something he had to chase anymore. It was happening around him, continuously.

Years passed. Marcus's finances grew more complex. He moved states. He added investments. He expanded his rental activity. Through it all, the AI adapted quietly in the background, adjusting to new rules, new jurisdictions, and new interpretations without drama. Marcus stopped waiting for the letter. He stopped worrying about surprises.

One evening, as he organized old paperwork he no longer needed, Marcus reflected on how much mental energy he had once spent fearing mistakes he didn't even understand. The letter he had dreaded for so long never came – not because he was lucky, but because he was protected.

Marcus realized then that true peace of mind doesn't come from knowing every rule. It comes from knowing that whatever changes, whatever shifts, and whatever evolves, someone — or something — is paying attention for you. With AI guarding compliance in real time, silence was no longer threatening. It was confirmation that everything was exactly as it should be.

Chapter 9

How AI Integrates Taxes, Financial Planning, and Long-Term Wealth Protection

For most people, taxes and financial planning exist in separate mental compartments. Taxes are something to survive once a year, while wealth planning is something to think about someday in the future. This separation is costly. Taxes are not just an annual expense; they are one of the largest forces shaping long-term wealth. Every decision about earning, saving, investing, spending, and transferring assets carries tax consequences that compound over time. Artificial intelligence closes this gap by integrating tax optimization directly into financial planning, transforming taxes from a recurring burden into a strategic lever for wealth protection and growth.

At the center of this integration is visibility across time. Traditional tax preparation focuses almost entirely on the past year. Financial planning, when it happens at all, often relies on generic assumptions that ignore tax friction. AI unifies these perspectives by maintaining a continuous model of your financial life across decades. It tracks income growth, asset appreciation, contribution limits, withdrawal rules, and tax law interactions simultaneously. This allows AI to evaluate not just whether a decision reduces taxes this year, but whether it strengthens or weakens your financial position ten, twenty, or thirty years into the future.

One of the most powerful applications of AI in this area is retirement planning. Contributions to retirement accounts affect current taxable income, future withdrawal taxes, eligibility for credits, and long-term cash flow. AI models these interactions dynamically. It can show when traditional contributions make sense versus Roth contributions, how contribution timing affects tax brackets, and how future required minimum distributions may impact retirement income. Instead of relying on static rules of thumb, AI builds a personalized strategy that evolves as your income, assets, and tax laws change.

AI also integrates tax planning with investment strategy. Asset location — deciding which investments belong in taxable accounts versus tax-advantaged accounts — can have a dramatic impact on long-term after-tax returns. AI evaluates the tax efficiency of each asset type and places it where it will generate the least drag. It coordinates capital gains planning, dividend taxation, loss harvesting, and rebalancing schedules in a way that minimizes tax leakage without sacrificing investment goals. Over time, these optimizations can mean the difference between financial security and financial stress.

Wealth protection extends beyond growth into risk management and legacy planning. Taxes affect how assets are transferred, inherited, and preserved across generations. AI tracks estate thresholds, gifting rules, step-up provisions, and beneficiary designations, ensuring that your plans remain aligned with current laws. It identifies opportunities to shift wealth efficiently while avoiding unnecessary exposure. This is not about avoiding taxes illegally — it is about structuring life decisions so that wealth is preserved rather than eroded.

AI also accounts for life transitions that often disrupt financial plans. Marriage, divorce, children, career changes, relocations, health events, and business ventures all alter tax and financial dynamics. AI adapts instantly to these changes, recalculating projections and adjusting strategies automatically. Instead of rebuilding plans from scratch after each life event, you have a system that evolves alongside you, maintaining continuity and coherence through change.

Another critical advantage of AI-driven integration is behavioral alignment. Humans struggle to balance short-term needs with long-term goals. AI provides clarity by showing the future impact of present choices. It translates abstract planning concepts into tangible outcomes, helping individuals make decisions that align with both current comfort and future security. This reduces impulsive decisions and replaces them with informed trade-offs.

Ultimately, AI transforms financial planning into a living process rather than a static document. Taxes are no longer something to minimize in isolation, but a variable that is continuously managed in service of long-term wealth protection. By integrating tax optimization with retirement planning, investment strategy, and legacy considerations, AI creates a financial ecosystem where every decision reinforces the next. Wealth is no longer built accidentally — it is built intentionally, intelligently, and sustainably.

The Plan That Finally Outlived the Fear

Helen had always been careful with money, but careful did not mean confident. She saved consistently, invested cautiously, and avoided unnecessary debt, yet she carried a constant fear that it wouldn't be enough. Every financial decision felt heavy, as if one wrong move could undo years of effort. Taxes, in particular, felt like a silent erosion she could never quite control. Each year she paid what she owed, told herself she was doing the right thing, and hoped the future would work itself out. Helen was in her early forties when the fear sharpened. Her parents were aging, her children were approaching college, and retirement no longer felt abstract.

She met with a financial planner who showed her charts and projections, but they felt detached from reality. The numbers assumed stable tax laws, steady markets, and perfect execution. Helen knew life was messier than that.

A colleague introduced her to an AI-powered financial and tax planning system, describing it as "a plan that updates itself." Skeptical but curious, Helen decided to try it. She connected her income, savings, investments, retirement accounts, and expenses. The system processed quietly, then presented something she had never seen before — a timeline of her financial life that accounted for taxes at every step.

The AI didn't just show her where she was. It showed her where she was *leaking*. It revealed how certain investment choices were creating unnecessary tax drag, how her retirement contributions could be structured more efficiently, and how future withdrawals might push her into higher tax brackets if nothing changed. None of it was alarming, but all of it was eye-opening.

What surprised Helen most was how the system treated time. It didn't fixate on this year's tax bill. It modeled how decisions compounded. It showed her how small optimizations now could preserve flexibility later. It illustrated different futures — one where she made no changes, one where she adjusted gradually, and one where her strategy aligned taxes and planning deliberately. The differences were profound.

As months passed, Helen began using the AI not as a calculator, but as a companion. Before increasing retirement contributions, she checked the long-term impact. When considering helping her parents financially, she explored how to do so tax-efficiently. When thinking about college savings, the system integrated education planning with tax benefits she hadn't fully understood before.

Life, as expected, didn't stay still. Helen changed jobs. Markets fluctuated. Tax rules shifted. Each time, the AI adapted quietly, recalculating projections without panic. The plan didn't break — it evolved. For the first time, Helen felt like her financial future wasn't balanced on fragile assumptions.

Years later, Helen sat at her kitchen table reviewing her updated plan. It wasn't perfect. No plan ever was. But it was resilient. It accounted for uncertainty instead of pretending it didn't exist. Taxes were no longer an invisible threat undermining her progress. They were a managed variable, woven into every decision.

Helen realized then that her fear had never been about money itself. It had been about *not knowing*. With AI integrating taxes and financial planning into one coherent system, the unknown had lost its grip. The future wasn't guaranteed – but it was navigable. And for the first time in her life, that was enough.

Chapter 10

The Future of AI-Powered Personal Taxes: From Annual Filing to Continuous Financial Autopilot

The future of personal taxation will not be defined by faster forms or prettier software interfaces. It will be defined by a fundamental shift in *when* taxes are managed, *how* decisions are made, and *who* truly controls the outcome. For more than a century, taxation has been treated as an annual event — something addressed retroactively, under pressure, with incomplete information. Artificial intelligence is ending that model permanently. In its place is a continuous, always-on tax intelligence layer that operates quietly in the background of everyday life, transforming taxes from a yearly obligation into a real-time financial control system.

In the coming years, filing a tax return will become the least important part of the tax process. AI systems already possess the ability to maintain a constantly updated tax profile that reflects income, expenses, assets, deductions, credits, and compliance status in real time. As governments modernize reporting infrastructure and financial platforms become increasingly interconnected, the act of "filing" will evolve into a confirmation rather than a construction. Returns will be largely pre-built, validated, and reconciled long before deadlines arrive. Stress will disappear not because taxes are simpler, but because they are never allowed to become unclear.

AI will also fundamentally change the relationship between taxpayers and tax authorities. Historically, this relationship has been adversarial by default, shaped by fear of audits, penalties, and enforcement. AI reframes compliance as alignment rather than confrontation. By ensuring that records are accurate, rules are followed, and documentation is preserved continuously, AI reduces friction on both sides. Tax authorities gain cleaner data and fewer disputes, while taxpayers gain confidence and predictability. This mutual transparency will redefine trust within the system.

Another defining feature of the future is personalization at scale. Tax systems have always been personalized in theory, but generalized in practice. AI enables truly individualized tax strategies that adapt to lifestyle, career choices, geography, family structure, and financial goals. Two people with identical incomes will no longer face identical tax outcomes if their behaviors differ. AI will recognize those differences instantly and optimize accordingly, ensuring that the tax code's incentives actually function as intended rather than being lost in complexity. Automation will also expand beyond optimization into prevention. AI systems will increasingly identify risky patterns before they result in penalties or audits. Instead of reacting to mistakes, systems will intervene early, guiding behavior toward safer, more compliant outcomes. This proactive protection will become one of the most valuable benefits of AI-powered taxation, especially as financial lives grow more complex and interconnected.

Perhaps the most profound shift will be psychological. For generations, taxes have been associated with anxiety, confusion, and helplessness. AI replaces these emotions with clarity and agency. When people can see the impact of decisions instantly, understand trade-offs clearly, and trust that no opportunity or obligation is being missed, taxes lose their emotional weight. They become just another managed variable — important, but no longer intimidating.

As AI continues to evolve, it will integrate even more deeply with broader financial ecosystems. Tax optimization will coordinate seamlessly with banking, investing, insurance, estate planning, and business operations. Financial decisions will no longer be evaluated in isolation. Every action will be understood within a unified framework designed to preserve wealth, minimize friction, and support long-term stability. The future of AI-powered personal taxes is not about paying less at all costs. It is about *knowing more at all times.* It is about replacing uncertainty with insight, reaction with intention, and fear with control. In that future, taxes will no longer be something people dread. They will be something people understand — and ultimately, something that quietly works for them instead of against them.

The Year Tax Season Disappeared

The year it happened, no one noticed at first.

There were no headlines announcing the end of tax season. No dramatic policy changes. No sudden breakthroughs splashed across the news. For Maya, it began as a quiet absence — the absence of a familiar tension that usually crept into her life sometime after the holidays. January arrived, then February, and something was missing. There was no knot in her stomach, no half-formed worry about documents she might have lost, no vague fear of what she might owe.

Maya was a product strategist by profession, but a realist by nature. She had spent most of her adult life navigating complexity carefully. She worked remotely, invested regularly, earned occasional side income, and supported her aging mother. Her finances were solid but layered, and taxes had always been the one area that made her feel perpetually behind. No matter how prepared she thought she was, there was always a surprise waiting.

Two years earlier, Maya had adopted an AI-powered financial and tax system after a particularly exhausting filing season. At the time, she saw it as a tool — something to reduce friction. She never imagined it would change her relationship with money entirely.

At first, the system felt almost invisible. It connected her accounts, tracked transactions, and offered the occasional notification. It wasn't loud or demanding. It didn't ask her to "do taxes." It simply watched, calculated, and adjusted. Over time, Maya began to rely on it the way one relies on a navigation app — not because she couldn't drive, but because there was no reason not to know the fastest, safest route.

As months passed, the AI quietly reshaped her experience of money. When Maya received a raise, the system recalculated her projected tax position instantly. When she helped her mother cover medical expenses, it flagged deductions and credits automatically. When she sold a small investment, it showed her how the timing affected both this year and the next. Nothing felt urgent. Nothing felt mysterious.

The real change came in December.

In previous years, December had been a month of internal bargaining. Should she prepay expenses? Increase retirement contributions? Delay income if possible? Each decision felt rushed and uncertain, based on incomplete information. This time, there was no scramble. The AI had been forecasting her tax position all year. It showed her, calmly and clearly, that she was exactly where she needed to be. No action required.

Maya waited for the familiar anxiety to arrive. It didn't.

January came. Then February. Friends began talking about gathering documents, scheduling appointments, bracing for surprises. Maya listened politely, then realized she had nothing to gather. Her return already existed — fully built, validated, and documented. Filing, when it happened, felt ceremonial rather than stressful. A confirmation, not a confrontation.

What startled Maya most was not how easy filing had become, but how much mental space had opened up in its absence. She hadn't realized how much energy she had spent *anticipating* tax stress year after year. Without it, her thoughts felt clearer. Decisions felt lighter. Money felt less like something to defend and more like something to direct.

One evening in early spring, Maya sat on her balcony watching the city settle into dusk. She thought about how quietly her financial life now operated. There were no dramatic swings, no sudden shocks, no lingering fear of mistakes. Everything adjusted gradually, predictably, almost gently. It occurred to her then that tax season hadn't ended because taxes no longer mattered. It had ended because taxes were finally being handled continuously, intelligently, and without drama. The system hadn't made her wealthier overnight. It had made her *steadier*. More confident. More present.

Maya smiled at the thought.

The future, she realized, doesn't always arrive with noise. Sometimes it arrives as silence — the silence of a problem that no longer exists, the silence of a fear that no longer has power. And in that silence, life feels just a little more free.

Final Thoughts

AI Personal Tax Optimization: How Artificial Intelligence Helps You Keep More of What You Earn

The story of taxes has always been a story of asymmetry. The system knows everything about the rules, while the individual knows very little. For decades, this imbalance has shaped how people experience taxation — as something confusing, intimidating, and reactive. What this book series has shown, from beginning to end, is that artificial intelligence permanently breaks that imbalance. Not by eliminating taxes, not by bypassing the law, but by restoring visibility, control, and intelligence to the individual for the first time in history.

AI-powered personal tax optimization is not just a technological upgrade. It is a structural correction. It replaces memory with data, guesswork with modeling, fear with clarity, and reaction with intention. Each chapter of this book has explored a different dimension of that transformation: how AI discovers deductions that humans miss, how it converts everyday spending into strategic assets, how it prevents overpayment before it happens, how it enforces accuracy with evidence rather than assumptions, how it coordinates decisions across an entire financial life, how it handles complex assets with precision, how it forecasts outcomes in real time, how it adapts instantly to legal change, how it integrates taxes into long-term wealth planning, and how it ultimately dissolves the very concept of "tax season" as we have always known it.

What becomes clear by the end is that the future of taxes is not about doing more work. It is about doing less — because the right system is doing the work for you. In an AI-driven model, compliance is not something you scramble to achieve. It is something that exists continuously. Optimization is not something you hope for at filing time. It is something that happens quietly every day. Protection is not something you react to after a notice arrives. It is built into the structure of your financial life from the beginning.

This matters not just for savings, but for peace of mind. Financial stress is rarely caused by lack of income alone. It is caused by uncertainty. By not knowing where you stand, what is coming, or whether you made the right decisions. AI removes that uncertainty by making outcomes visible before they arrive. When you can see the future impact of your choices, fear loses its power. Taxes stop being a looming threat and become a manageable variable within a larger, intelligent system.

Equally important is what AI does *not* do. It does not replace human judgment, values, or goals. It does not tell you what kind of life to live. Instead, it supports your decisions by ensuring that whatever path you choose is navigated with maximum efficiency and minimum friction. Whether you value stability, growth, flexibility, legacy, or freedom, AI aligns the tax system with those priorities rather than working against them.

As governments modernize, financial platforms interconnect, and AI systems grow more sophisticated, the direction is clear. The old model of annual stress, reactive filing, and constant uncertainty will not survive. It cannot compete with a system that operates continuously, learns constantly, and adapts instantly. The individuals who embrace this shift early will not just save money — they will gain confidence, clarity, and control that compound year after year.

The purpose of this book was never simply to explain AI tax tools. It was to change how you think about taxes entirely. To show that taxation does not have to be something you endure, fear, or avoid thinking about. With the right intelligence in place, taxes become something you understand, plan for, and integrate seamlessly into a well-designed financial life.

The future of personal taxes is not louder, faster, or more complicated. It is quieter, clearer, and more humane. And it is already here.

www.ingramcontent.com/pod-product-compliance
Lightning Source LLC
LaVergne TN
LVHW022023200926
848481LV00007B/2501